Keep little hands and minds busy with fun farm animals and fanciful fairies. With each side presenting a new scene, you and your baby will have hours of learning and play.

2 Basic Square

4 Farm Block

24 Fairy Princess Block

43 General Instructions

48 Yarn Information

Basic Square

Finished Size:
6½" (16.5 cm) square

GAUGE INFORMATION

Gauge Swatch: 3" (7.5 cm) square
Work same as Basic Square through Rnd 7: 48 sc and 4 corner ch-2 sps.

Rnd 1 (Right side)**:** With color indicated in individual instructions and using an adjustable loop to form a ring ***(Figs. 1a-d, page 46)***, work 8 sc in ring; do **not** join, place marker to indicate beginning of rnd ***(see Markers, page 44)***.

Note: Loop a short piece of yarn around any stitch to mark Rnd 1 as **right** side.

Rnd 2: (Ch 2, sc in next 2 sc) 4 times: 8 sc and 4 corner ch-2 sps.

Rnd 3: ★ (Sc, ch 2, sc) in next corner ch-2 sp, sc in next 2 sc; repeat from ★ around: 16 sc and 4 corner ch-2 sps.

Rnds 4-15: ★ Sc in each sc across to next corner ch-2 sp, (sc, ch 2, sc) in corner ch-2 sp; repeat from ★ around, sc in each sc across: 112 sc and 4 corner ch-2 sps.

Slip st in next sc; finish off.

JOINING

With **wrong** sides together and using Diagram as a guide for placement, join 4 Squares to center Square as follows:

With color indicated in individual instructions and working through **both** loops of sc on **both** pieces, join yarn with sc in any corner ch-2 sp ***(see Joining With Sc, page 45)***; sc in each sc across to next corner ch-2 sp, sc in corner ch-2 sp, ★ working through **both** loops of sc on **next** Square and center Square, sc in same corner ch-2 sp as last sc on center Square and in any corner ch-2 sp on next Square, sc in each sc across to next corner ch-2 sp, sc in corner ch-2 sp; repeat from ★ 2 times **more**, ending by working last sc in same corner ch-2 sp on center Square as first sc; join with slip st to first sc, finish off.

Using remaining Square as center on Fairy Princess Block **only**, repeat Joining around opposite sides of Squares.

Fairy Princess Block Side Seam

With **wrong** sides together and working through **both** loops of sts across any unjoined edge, join Purple with sc in any corner ch-2 sp; sc in each sc across to next corner ch-2 sp, sc in corner ch-2 sp; finish off.

Repeat Side Seam across each unjoined edge, stuffing Block with polyester fiberfill before closing.

Thread upholstery needle with a long strand of Square color yarn. Sew through middle of one Square and come out through middle of Square on opposite side of Block twice. Secure ends.

Repeat with remaining Squares of Block.

DIAGRAM

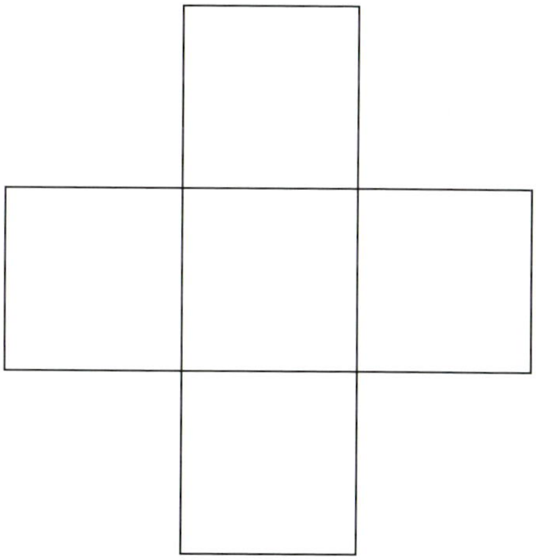

Farm Block

EASY

Finished Size:
Approximately 6½" (16.5 cm) cube

SHOPPING LIST

Yarn (Medium Weight) MEDIUM 4

[7 ounces, 364 yards
(198 grams, 333 meters) per skein]:

- ☐ Red - 1 skein
- ☐ Grey - 85 yards (77.5 meters)
- ☐ Lt Blue - 60 yards (55 meters)
- ☐ White - 45 yards (41 meters)
- ☐ Black - 25 yards (23 meters)
- ☐ Dk Brown - 25 yards (23 meters)
- ☐ Gold - 25 yards (23 meters)
- ☐ Lt Green - 15 yards (13.5 meters)
- ☐ Green - 15 yards (13.5 meters)
- ☐ Brown - 15 yards (13.5 meters)
- ☐ Lt Pink - small amount
- ☐ Pink - small amount
- ☐ Yellow - small amount
- ☐ Lt Yellow - small amount
- ☐ Tan - small amount
- ☐ Orange - small amount

[5 ounces, 236 yards,
(141 grams, 215 meters) per skein]:

- ☐ Variegated - small amount

Crochet Hook

- ☐ Size H (5 mm)
  or size needed for gauge

Additional Supplies

- ☐ Yarn needle
- ☐ Upholstery needle
- ☐ Polyester fiberfill

STITCH GUIDE

SINGLE CROCHET 2 TOGETHER *(abbreviated sc2tog)*

Pull up a loop in each of next 2 sc, YO and draw through all 3 loops on hook (**counts as one sc**).

Block

BLOCK

Make 4 Red Squares (sides) and one Lt Blue Square (bottom) ***(see Basic Square, page 2)***.

With White, work Joining to attach Red Squares to Lt Blue Square.

When **right** or **wrong** side is indicated, loop a short piece of yarn around any stitch on same row or rnd **(now and throughout)**.

Use photos as guides for placement of all pieces. For embroidery, refer to Figs. 4-7, page 47.

LOFT

Row 1: With **right** side facing, join Red with slip st in first sc on top edge of any Side; ch 1, beginning in same sc, sc2tog, sc in next 24 sc, sc2tog: 26 sc.

Row 2: Ch 1, turn; sc in each sc across.

Row 3 (Decrease row)**:** Ch 1, turn; beginning in first sc, sc2tog, sc in each sc across to last 2 sc, sc2tog: 24 sc.

Row 4: Ch 1, turn; sc in each sc across.

Rows 5 and 6: Repeat Row 3 twice: 20 sc.

Rows 7-9: Ch 1, turn; beginning in first sc, sc2tog twice, sc in each sc across to last 4 sc, sc2tog twice: 8 sc.

Rows 10-12: Ch 1, turn; beginning in first sc, sc2tog across; at end of Row 12, finish off.

Side Seam: With **wrong** sides of Loft Square and side Square together, and working through **both** loops of sc on **both** pieces, join White with sc in first sc at bottom corner; sc in each sc across to next corner ch-2 sp, sc in corner ch-2 sp; sc evenly across ends of rows on Loft to next corner ch-2 sp, sc in corner ch-2 sp; with **wrong** sides of Loft Square and next side Square together, working through **both** loops of sc on **both** pieces, sc in each sc across; finish off.

Work Loft and Side Seam on opposite Square.

Thread upholstery needle with a long strand of Red. Sew through middle of one Square and come out through middle of Square on opposite side of Block twice. Secure ends.

Repeat with remaining Squares of Block.

ROOF

LOWER PANEL

With Grey, ch 9.

Row 1 (Wrong side)**:** Sc in second ch from hook and in each ch across: 8 sc.

Rows 2-30: Ch 1, turn; sc in each sc across; at end of Row 30, finish off.

UPPER PANEL

With Grey, ch 11.

Row 1 (Wrong side)**:** Sc in second ch from hook and in each ch across: 10 sc.

Rows 2-30: Ch 1, turn; sc in each sc across.

Do **not** finish off.

Joining: Holding Upper and Lower Panels with **wrong** sides together and beginning chs at same end, sc evenly across ends of rows; finish off.

Work a second Upper Panel and join it to first Upper Panel in same manner.

Work a second Lower Panel; at end of Row 30, do **not** finish off. Join second Lower Panel to second Upper Panel in same manner.

With **wrong** sides together, working in free loops of beginning chs on Panels *(Fig. 2b, page 46)* and in **both** loops of sc on all pieces, join White with sc in any st; sc in each st and in end of each row across stuffing Block with polyester fiberfill before closing; join with slip st to first sc; finish off.

FRONT

DOORWAY

Row 1 (Wrong side)**:** With Dk Brown, work 20 fsc ***(see Foundation Single Crochet, page 45)***.

Rows 2-16: Ch 1, turn: sc in each st across; at end of Row 16, finish off leaving a long end.

Sew Doorway to Front, with ends of rows of Doorway at bottom edge of Square.

LARGE POCKET

Row 1 (Right side)**:** With Gold, work 20 fsc.

Rows 2-9: Ch 1, turn; sc in each st across; at end of Row 9, finish off leaving a long end.

Centering Large Pocket across Doorway, sew to bottom edge of Square working across 3 sides and leaving top edge free.

WINDOW

With Black, ch 11.

Row 1 (Right side)**:** Sc in second ch from hook and in each ch across: 10 sc.

Rows 2-6: Ch 1, turn; sc in each sc across; at end of Row 6, finish off.

Edging: With **right** side facing, join White with sc in first sc; ch 2, sc in same st and in next 8 sc, (sc, ch 2, sc) in last sc; sc in end of next 5 rows; working in free loops of beginning ch, (sc, ch 2, sc) in first ch, sc in next 8 chs, (sc, ch 2, sc) in next ch; sc in end of next 5 rows; join with slip st to first sc, finish off leaving a long end.

With **right** side facing, sew Back Loops Only of Edging to Square ***(Fig. 3, page 46)***, centered over Doorway.

HAY POCKET

With Gold, ch 11.

Row 1 (Wrong side)**:** Sc in second ch from hook and in each ch across: 10 sc.

Rows 2-4: Ch 1, turn; sc in each sc across; at end of Row 4, finish off leaving a long end.

With **right** side facing, sew Hay Pocket to inner and bottom edges of Window leaving top edge free.

DOOR (Make 2)

With Red, ch 19.

Row 1: Dc in third ch from hook and in each ch across to last ch, (dc, ch 2, 3 dc, ch 2, dc) in last ch; working in free loops of beginning ch, dc in next 16 chs; do **not** join: 37 dc and 2 ch-2 sps.

Row 2 (Right side)**:** Ch 3 **(counts as first dc, now and throughout)**, turn; dc in next 16 dc, (2 dc, ch 2, 2 dc) in next ch-2 sp, dc in next 3 dc, (2 dc, ch 2, 2 dc) in next ch-2 sp, dc in last 17 dc; finish off: 45 dc and 2 ch-2 sps.

Edging: With **right** side facing, join White with sc in first dc; ch 2, sc in same dc, ★ sc in each dc across to next ch-2 sp, (sc, ch 2, sc) in ch-2 sp; repeat from ★ once **more**, sc in each dc across to last dc, (sc, ch 2, sc) in last dc; work 7 sc evenly spaced across ends of rows; join with slip st to first sc, finish off leaving a long end.

DOOR "X" (Make 2)

With White and leaving a long end, ch 23; finish off leaving a long end.

Sew chs to Door forming an X.

With **right** side facing, sew long edge of each Door to Square with opposite long edge centered on Doorway.

Side 1

SIDE 1

TREE TRUNK

Row 1 (Right side)**:** With Dk Brown, make 15 fhdc ***(see Foundation Half Double Crochet, page 45)***; finish off leaving a long end.

With **right** side facing, sew Tree Trunk to Square with end of row at bottom edge.

LEAVES

Rnd 1 (Right side)**:** With Green, ch 3; 11 dc in third ch from hook; join with slip st to top of beginning ch: 12 sts.

Rnd 2: Ch 3, dc in same st as joining, 2 dc in next dc and in each dc around; join with slip st to first dc, finish off leaving a long end: 24 dc.

With **right** side facing, sew Leaves to top of Tree Trunk.

WINDOW (Make 2)

Rnd 1 (Right side)**:** With Black and using an adjustable loop to form a ring; work 8 sc in ring; join with slip st to first sc.

Rnd 2: Ch 1, sc in same st as joining and in next sc, ch 2, (sc in next 2 sc, ch 2) 3 times; join with slip st to first sc, finish off: 8 sc and 4 ch-2 sps.

Edging: With **right** side facing, join White with sc in any ch-2 sp; ch 2, sc in same sp and in next 2 sc, ★ (sc, ch 2, sc) in next ch-2 sp, sc in next 2 sc; repeat from ★ 2 times **more**; join with slip st to first sc, finish off leaving a long end.

With White and using straight st, add panes.

With **right** side facing, sew Back Loops Only of Window Edgings to Square.

FENCE

POST (Make 4)

With White, ch 9.

Row 1 (Right side)**:** Hdc in second ch from hook and in each ch across; finish off leaving a long end: 8 hdc.

UPPER RAIL

With **wrong** side facing, join White with slip st around third hdc on any Post; ★ ch 5, with **right** side facing, slip st in beginning ch at base of third hdc on **next** Post, ch 1, with **wrong** side of same Post facing, slip st around **same** hdc; repeat from ★ 2 times **more**; finish off.

LOWER RAIL

Working around sixth hdc on each Post, work same as Upper Rail.

Sew bottom edge of each Post to Square, then sew long edges of end Posts to Square leaving Rails unattached. Sew top of center Posts in place.

Back

BACK
LARGE WINDOW

With Black, ch 11.

Row 1 (Right side)**:** Sc in second ch from hook and in each ch across: 10 sc.

Rows 2-10: Ch 1, turn; sc in each sc across; at end of Row 10, finish off.

Edging: With **right** side facing, join White with sc in end of first row, sc in end of next 8 rows; (sc, ch 2, sc) in first sc, sc in next 8 sc, (sc, ch 2, sc) in last sc, sc in end of next 9 rows; finish off leaving a long end.

POCKET

With Red, work same as Large Window through Row 4; at end of Row 4, finish off leaving a long end: 10 sc.

Edging: With **right** side facing, join White with sc in first sc; sc in each sc across; finish off.

With **right** side facing and using White end, sew bottom of Window and Edging to Square, tacking each end of Pocket Edging to sc on each side of Window Edging. Using Red end, sew sides and bottom of Pocket to Square.

SMALL WINDOW

With Black, ch 11.

Row 1 (Right side)**:** Sc in second ch from hook and in each ch across: 10 sc.

Rows 2-4: Ch 1, turn; sc in each sc across; at end of Row 4, finish off.

Row 5: With **right** side facing and working in Back Loops Only, join Gold with sc in first sc; sc in each sc across.

Row 6: Ch 1, turn; sc in Front Loop Only of each sc across; finish off.

Edging: With **right** side facing and working in Back Loops Only, join White with sc in first sc; ch 2, sc in same st and in next 8 sc, (sc, ch 2, sc) in last sc; sc in end of next 5 rows; working in free loops of beginning ch, (sc, ch 2, sc) in first ch, sc in next 8 chs, (sc, ch 2, sc) in next ch; sc in end of first 5 rows; join with slip st to first sc, finish off leaving a long end.

With **right** side facing, sew Back Loops Only of Small Window Edging to Square.

Tie short pieces of Gold to free loops of each sc on Rows 4-6 ***(Fig. 2a, page 46)*** for hay. Trim ends.

Side 2

SIDE 2
GRASS

With Lt Green, ch 20.

Row 1 (Right side)**:** Dc in fourth ch from hook and in each ch across; finish off leaving a long end.

With **right** side facing, sew Grass to bottom edge of Square working around 3 sides, leaving top edge free.

WINDOW (Make 2)

Rnd 1 (Right side)**:** With Black, ch 3, 2 dc in third ch from hook, ch 2, (3 dc in same st, ch 2) 3 times; join with slip st to top of beginning ch: 12 sts and 4 corner ch-2 sps.

Rnd 2: Ch 3, dc in next 2 dc, (2 dc, ch 2, 2 dc) in next corner ch-2 sp, ★ dc in next 3 dc, (2 dc, ch 2, 2 dc) in next corner ch-2 sp; repeat from ★ 2 times **more**; join with slip st to first dc, finish off: 28 dc and 4 corner ch-2 sps.

Edging: With **right** side facing, join White with sc in any corner ch-2 sp; ch 2, sc in same sp and in next 7 dc, ★ (sc, ch 2, sc) in next corner ch-2 sp, sc in next 7 dc; repeat from ★ 2 times **more**; join with slip st to first sc, finish off leaving a long end: 36 sc and 4 corner ch-2 sps.

With **right** side facing, sew Back Loops Only of Window Edgings to Square.

HAY POCKET (Make 2)

With Gold, ch 10.

Row 1 (Wrong side)**:** Sc in second ch from hook and in each ch across: 9 sc.

Rows 2-4: Ch 1, turn; sc in each sc across; at end of Row 4, finish off leaving a long end.

With **right** side facing, sew Hay Pocket to inner and bottom edges of Window, working across 3 sides.

BASKET

SIDE (Make 2)

Row 1: With Brown, ch 3, 5 dc in third ch from hook; do **not** join: 6 sts.

Row 2 (Right side)**:** Ch 3, turn; dc in first st, 2 dc in each of last 5 sts; ch 2, work 7 sc evenly spaced across ends of rows; finish off leaving a long end on one Side only.

With **wrong** sides together and matching sts, sew across dc of Row 2 only.

Handle: With **right** side facing, join Brown with slip st in center ch of Row 1 on one Side; ch 12, slip st in center ch on second Side; finish off.

With Red and leaving a long end, ch 40 **tightly**; finish off leaving a long end.

Sew one end of ch to side of Square. Slide Basket Handle onto ch; sew second end of ch to opposite side of Square.

EGG (Make 2)

Rnd 1 (Right side)**:** With White and using an adjustable loop to form a ring, work 6 sc in ring; 3 sc in first sc, slip st in next sc, finish off.

CHICK (Make 2)

With Yellow, work same as Egg.

With Orange and using straight st, add beak and feet to Chick. With Black and using straight st, add eyes.

With **wrong** sides of one Egg and one Chick together, sew pieces together working through inside loops only on Egg and both loops of Chick.

Repeat with remaining Egg and Chick.

Join Black with slip st in st at edge of Egg; ch 50 **tightly**; slip st in any st on inside of Basket; finish off.

Repeat with second Egg.

BOTTOM

BACK FIELD

Row 1: With Green, work 20 fdc ***(see Foundation Double Crochet, page 45)***.

Rows 2 and 3: Ch 3, turn; dc in next st and in each st across.

Row 4: Ch 3, turn; dc in next 8 dc, hdc in next 2 dc, sc in last 9 dc.

Row 5 (Right side)**:** Ch 1, turn; sc in first 9 sc, hdc in next 2 hdc, dc in last 9 dc.

Row 6: Ch 2 (**counts as first hdc**), turn; hdc in next 2 dc, dc in next 5 dc, hdc in next 4 sts, sc in last 8 sc; finish off leaving a long end.

FRONT FIELD

With Lt Green, work same as Back Field through Row 3: 20 dc.

Row 4: Ch 1, turn; 2 sc in first dc, sc in next 10 dc, hdc in next 2 dc, dc in last 7 dc: 21 sts.

Row 5 (Right side)**:** Ch 3, turn; , dc in next 3 dc, hdc in next 2 dc, sc in next 9 sts, slip st in next sc, leave remaining sc unworked; finish off.

MUD PUDDLE

TOP

With Brown, ch 17.

Row 1 (Right side)**:** Sc in second ch from hook and in each ch across; finish off leaving a long end.

BOTTOM

With Brown, ch 17.

Row 1 (Right side)**:** Dc in third ch from hook and in each ch across; finish off leaving a long end.

With **right** sides facing, sew Top in a curve to Front Field; then sew each end of Bottom to Top. Sew first and last 3 dc of Bottom to Front Field leaving the remaining sts free.

With **right** sides facing, place both Fields on Square, placing top edge of Front Field over bottom edge of Back Field. Sew Fields to Square, working across 3 sides on each Field and leaving top edges free.

SUNFLOWER

CENTER

Rnd 1 (Right side)**:** With Dk Brown and using an adjustable loop to form a ring, work 6 sc in ring; join with slip st to first sc, finish off leaving a long end.

With **right** side facing, sew Back Loops Only of Center to Square.

With Lt Yellow and using lazy daisy st, add petals.

With Lt Green, add stem using backstitch and leaves using lazy daisy st.

SUN

Rnd 1 (Right side)**:** With Yellow and using an adjustable loop to form a ring, ch 1, work 12 dc in ring; join with slip st to first dc, finish off leaving a long end.

With **right** side facing, sew Sun to Square.

With Orange and using straight st, add rays.

FINGER PUPPETS

BASIC BODY (Make 2)

Rnd 1 (Right side)**:** With color indicated, ch 3, 11 dc in third ch from hook; join with slip st to top of beginning ch: 12 sts.

Rnd 2: Skip next dc, 6 dc in next dc (head), skip next dc, slip st in next dc; finish off leaving remaining dc unworked.

With **wrong** sides together and matching sts, sew pieces together leaving bottom 4 dc free.

CHICKEN

With White, make Basic Body.

WINGS & TAIL (Make 3)

With White, ch 1, **tightly** ch 5, slip st in first ch, (**tightly** ch 6, slip st in same ch) twice; finish off leaving a long end.

Sew a Wing to each side of Body and Tail to bottom of Rnd 1.

Comb: With Red, **tightly** ch 3; finish off leaving a long end.

Sew Comb to top of head.

With Black and using straight st, add eyes. With Yellow and using satin st, add beak and feet.

ROOSTER

With Brown, make Basic Body.

WINGS & TAIL (Make 3)

With Variegated, work same as Chicken Wings & Tail.

Work Comb same as Chicken.

With Black and using straight st, add eyes. With Yellow and using satin st, add beak and feet. With Red and using straight st, add wattle.

SHEEP

With White, make Basic Body.

EAR (Make 2)

Row 1 (Right side)**:** With Tan, ch 3, sc in second ch from hook, hdc in last ch; finish off leaving a long end.

Muzzle (Right side)**:** With Tan and using an adjustable loop to form a ring, work 8 sc in ring; join with slip st to first sc.

Sew Ears to top of head. Sew Muzzle to head and Body.

With Black and using straight st, add eyes and mouth. With Tan and using satin st, add hooves.

PIG

With Lt Pink, make Basic Body.

EAR (Make 2)

Row 1 (Right side)**:** With Pink, ch 3, sc in second ch from hook and in last ch; finish off leaving a long end.

Finger Puppets

Snout (Right side)**:** With Pink and using an adjustable loop to form a ring, work 6 sc in ring; join with slip st to first sc; finish off leaving a long end.

Sew Ears to top of head. Sew Snout to head and Body.

With Black and using straight st, add eyes and nostrils. With Pink and using satin st, add hooves. With Pink and using backstitch, add tail.

COW

With White, make Basic Body.

EAR (Make 2)

Row 1 (Right side)**:** With Black, ch 4, sc in second ch from hook, hdc in next ch, sc in last ch; finish off leaving a long end.

Eye Patch: With Black, ch 2, 4 sc in second ch from hook; finish off leaving a long end.

Muzzle (Right side)**:** With Lt Pink and using an adjustable loop to form a ring, work 6 sc in ring; join with slip st to first sc, finish off leaving a long end.

Spot: With Black, work same as Muzzle.

Tail: With White, **tightly** ch 3; finish off leaving a long end.

Sew Ears and Eye Patch to head. Sew Muzzle to Body overlapping Eye Patch. Sew Spot and Tail to back. With Black and using straight st, add one eye and nostrils. With White and using straight st, add eye to Eye Patch. With Grey and using satin st, add hooves.

HORSE

With Brown, make Basic Body.

EAR (Make 2)

With Brown, work same as Cow.

Muzzle (Right side)**:** With Tan and using an adjustable loop to form a ring, work 6 sc in ring; join with slip st to first sc, finish off leaving a long end.

Mane: With Black, ch 5; finish off leaving a long end.

Tail

With Black, ch 8; slip st at center back of Body, ch 7; finish off.

With Black, ch 6; slip st in same st at back of Body; finish off.

Tie a knot at end of each ch; trim short.

Sew Ears and Mane to top of head. Sew Muzzle to Body. With Black and using straight st, add eyes. With Dk Brown and using straight st, add nostrils and mouth. With Dk Brown and using satin st, add hooves.

Fairy Princess Block

EASY

Finished Size:
Approximately 6½" (16.5 cm) cube

SHOPPING LIST

Yarn (Medium Weight) MEDIUM 4

[7 ounces, 364 yards
(198 grams, 333 meters) per skein]:

- ☐ Lt Pink - 65 yards (59.5 meters)
- ☐ Pink - 65 yards (59.5 meters)
- ☐ Lt Blue - 60 yards (55 meters)
- ☐ Blue - 60 yards (55 meters)
- ☐ Navy - 60 yards (55 meters)
- ☐ Lt Purple - 60 yards (55 meters)
- ☐ Purple - 30 yards (27.5 meters)
- ☐ White - 25 yards (23 meters)
- ☐ Grey - 15 yards (13.5 meters)
- ☐ Lt Yellow - 15 yards (13.5 meters)
- ☐ Lt Green - 10 yards (9 meters)
- ☐ Green - 10 yards (9 meters)
- ☐ Dk Brown - 10 yards (9 meters)
- ☐ Red - 10 yards (9 meters)
- ☐ Black - 10 yards (9 meters)
- ☐ Lt Jade - small amount
- ☐ Jade - small amount

[5 ounces, 236 yards,
(141 grams, 215 meters) per skein]:

- ☐ Variegated - small amount

Crochet Hook

- ☐ Size H (5 mm)
  or size needed for gauge

Additional Supplies

- ☐ Yarn needle
- ☐ Upholstery needle
- ☐ Polyester fiberfill
- ☐ Hole punch
- ☐ Flexible mirror sheet
- ☐ Rattle
- ☐ 5/8" (16 mm) organdy ribbon - 1 yard (1 meter)
- ☐ Tapestry needle and Black embroidery floss (Finger Puppets only)

STITCH GUIDE

TREBLE CROCHET *(abbreviated tr)*

YO twice, insert hook in st indicated, YO and pull up a loop (4 loops on hook), (YO and draw through 2 loops on hook) 3 times.

SINGLE CROCHET 2 TOGETHER *(abbreviated sc2tog)*

Pull up a loop in each of next 2 sts, YO and draw through all 3 loops on hook **(counts as one sc)**.

DOUBLE CROCHET 2 TOGETHER *(abbreviated dc2tog)* (uses next 2 sts)

★ YO, insert hook in **next** st, YO and pull up a loop, YO and draw through 2 loops on hook; repeat from ★ once **more**, YO and draw through all 3 loops on hook **(counts as one dc)**.

BLOCK

Make 6 Squares: One **each** Lt Purple (Top), Pink (Bottom), Blue (Side 1), Lt Pink (Side 2), Navy (Side 3), and Lt Blue (Side 4) ***(see Basic Square, page 2)***.

With Purple, work Joining and Side Seams.

When **right** side is indicated, loop a short piece of yarn around any stitch on same row or rnd **(now and throughout)**.

Use photos as guides for placement of all pieces. For embroidery, refer to Figs. 4-7, page 47.

TOP

CASTLE

FRONT

With Grey, ch 12.

Row 1 (Right side)**:** Dc in third ch from hook and in each ch across to last ch, (dc, ch 2, 3 dc, ch 2, dc) in last ch; working in free loops of beginning ch ***(Fig. 2b, page 46)***, dc in next 10 chs; do **not** join: 25 sts and 2 ch-2 sps.

Row 2: Ch 3 **(counts as first dc, now and throughout)**, turn; dc in next 10 dc, (2 dc, ch 2, 2 dc) in next ch-2 sp, dc in next 3 dc, (2 dc, ch 2, 2 dc) in next ch-2 sp, dc in last 11 sts; finish off leaving a long end: 33 dc.

Top

DOORWAY

With Black, ch 6.

Row 1 (Right side)**:** Hdc in third ch from hook and in next 2 chs, 5 hdc in last ch; working in free loops of beginning ch, hdc in next 3 chs; do **not** join: 12 sts.

Row 2: Ch 2 (**counts as first hdc**), turn; hdc in next 2 hdc, 2 hdc in each of next 5 hdc, hdc in last 4 sts; finish off leaving a long end: 17 hdc.

Sew Doorway to Castle Front.

SMALL TOWER (Make 2)

With Grey, ch 10.

Row 1 (Right side)**:** Dc in third ch from hook and in each ch across to last ch, (dc, ch 2, 3 dc, ch 2, dc) in last ch; working in free loops of beginning ch, dc in next 8 chs; do **not** join, finish off leaving a long end: 21 sts.

With **wrong** sides together and bottom edges at same end, sew a Tower to each side of Castle.

TOWER WINDOW (Make 2)

Row 1 (Right side)**:** With Black, ch 3, sc in second ch from hook and in last ch; finish off leaving a long end.

Sew Windows to Towers.

Sew Castle to Square, with bottom edge at third rnd up from bottom edge of Square.

CASTLE ROOF

Row 1 (Right side)**:** With Purple, ch 3, 2 dc in third ch from hook: 3 sts.

Row 2: Ch 3, turn; dc in first dc, 2 dc in each of last 2 sts: 6 dc.

Row 3: Ch 3, turn; 2 dc in next dc, (dc in next dc, 2 dc in next dc) twice: 9 dc.

Row 4: Ch 3, turn; dc in next dc, 2 dc in next dc, (dc in next 2 dc, 2 dc in next dc) twice: 12 dc.

Row 5: Ch 1, turn; sc in next dc and in each dc across; finish off leaving a long end.

Sew Roof to Square, overlapping top edge of Castle Front.

TOWER ROOF (Make 2)

Row 1 (Right side)**:** With Purple, ch 3, 2 dc in third ch from hook: 3 sts.

Row 2: Ch 3, turn; dc in first dc, 2 dc in each of last 2 sts: 6 dc.

Row 3: Ch 1, turn; 2 sc in first dc, sc in next 2 dc, 2 sc in next dc, sc in last 2 dc; finish off leaving a long end: 8 sc.

Sew each Roof to Square, overlapping top edge of each Small Tower.

SMALL FLAG (Make 2)

With Lt Pink, ch 3.

Row 1: Sc in second ch from hook, dc in last ch; finish off leaving a long end.

Sew one Small Flag to top of each Tower Roof.

LARGE FLAG

With Lt Pink, ch 6.

Row 1: Slip st in second ch from hook, sc in next ch, hdc in next ch, dc in last 2 chs; finish off leaving a long end.

Sew Large Flag to top of Castle Roof.

CLOUD

With White, ch 19.

Row 1 (Right side)**:** 3 Dc in third ch from hook, dc in next 15 chs, 4 dc in last ch: 23 sts.

Row 2: Turn; slip st in first 6 dc, (skip next dc, 3 dc in next dc) twice, skip next dc, sc in next dc, (skip next dc, 3 dc in next dc) twice, skip next dc, slip st in next dc, leave remaining sts unworked: 12 dc and one sc.

Row 3: Turn; slip st in next 5 dc, skip next dc, 6 tr in next sc, skip next dc, slip st in next dc, leave remaining sts unworked; finish off leaving a long end.

Sew bottom and side edges of Cloud across bottom edge of Square.

With White and using straight st, add stars.

Side 1

SIDE 1 UNICORN

NECK

With White, ch 11.

Row 1 (Right side)**:** Dc in third ch from hook and in next 7 chs, 5 dc in last ch; working in free loops of beginning ch, dc in next 8 chs: 21 dc.

Edging Rnd: Ch 3, do **not** turn; work 4 dc evenly spaced across end of Row 1, ch 2, dc in first 9 dc, ch 2, 2 dc in next dc, (dc, ch 2, dc) in next dc, 2 dc in next dc, ch 2, dc in last 9 dc, ch 2; join with slip st to first dc, finish off leaving a long end.

MUZZLE

Rnd 1 (Right side)**:** With White, ch 3, 11 dc in third ch from hook; join with slip st to top of beginning ch, finish off.

HEAD

Rnd 1 (Right side)**:** With White, ch 3, 11 dc in third ch from hook; join with slip st to top of beginning ch: 12 sts.

Rnd 2: Ch 3, dc in same st as joining, 2 dc in each dc around; join with slip st to first dc: 24 dc.

Joining Rnd: Sc in same st as joining, hdc in next dc, dc in next dc; with **right** side of Muzzle facing, sc in any dc, 2 sc in next dc, (sc in next dc, 2 sc in next dc) twice, hdc in next dc, dc in next dc, leave remaining dc unworked; skip next 3 dc on Head and slip st in next dc, finish off leaving a long end.

EAR (Make 2)

With White, ch 7.

Row 1 (Right side)**:** Slip st in second ch from hook, sc in next ch, hdc in next ch, dc in next ch, hdc in next ch, 3 sc in last ch; working in free loops of beginning ch, hdc in next ch, dc in next ch, hdc in next ch, sc in next ch, slip st in next ch; finish off leaving a long end.

HORN

With Grey, ch 9.

Row 1 (Right side)**:** Slip st in second ch from hook and in next ch, sc in next 2 chs, hdc in next 2 chs, dc in last 2 chs; finish off leaving a long end.

EYE

With Black, ch 3, 3 dc in third ch from hook; finish off leaving a long end.

Sew Eye to Head.

With Black and using backstitch, add mouth. With Black and using straight st, add nostril.

Sew Ears to Head, placing end of one Ear behind Head. Sew Horn to forehead.

Sew Neck to Blue Square, placing center ch-2 sp in bottom right corner.

Sew space between Head and Muzzle closed, then sew Back Loops Only of piece to Square, overlapping Neck and leaving top edge of front Ear free.

Cut twenty, 6" (15 cm) strands of Variegated and tie center of strands to top of Head and back of Neck for mane. Trim ends.

SIDE 2

POCKET

With Lt Pink, ch 10.

Row 1: Dc in third ch from hook and in each ch across to last ch, 6 dc in last ch; working in free loops of beginning ch, dc in next 8 chs; do **not** join: 22 sts.

Row 2 (Right side)**:** Ch 3, turn; dc in next 7 dc, 2 dc in each of next 6 dc, dc in last 8 sts: 28 dc.

Row 3: Ch 3, turn; dc in next 8 dc, 2 dc in next dc, (dc in next dc, 2 dc in next dc) 5 times, dc in last 8 dc: 34 dc.

Row 4: Ch 3, turn; dc in next 8 dc, 2 dc in next dc, (dc in next 2 dc, 2 dc in next dc) 5 times, dc in last 9 dc: 40 dc.

Edging: Ch 1, do **not** turn; work 16 sc evenly spaced across ends of rows; finish off leaving a long end.

With **right** side facing, sew Pocket to Lt Pink Square.

WAND RATTLE

STAR

CENTER

Rnd 1 (Right side)**:** With Yellow and using an adjustable loop to form a ring, work 6 sc in ring; place marker to indicate beginning of rnd.

Rnd 2: 2 Sc in each sc around: 12 sc.

Rnd 3: (Sc in next sc, 2 sc in next sc) around: 18 sc.

Rnd 4: (Sc in next 2 sc, 2 sc in next sc) around: 24 sc.

Rnds 5-7: Sc in each sc around.

Rnd 8: (Sc2tog, sc in next 2 sc) around: 18 sc.

Stuff Star with polyester fiberfill, placing rattle in center.

Rnd 9: Sc2tog around: 9 sc.

Continue to sc2tog until hole is closed; finish off.

POINT (Make 5)

Rnd 1 (Right side)**:** With Yellow and using an adjustable loop to form a ring, work 6 sc in ring; place marker to indicate beginning of rnd.

Rnds 2 and 3: Sc in each sc around.

Rnd 4: 2 Sc in each sc around: 12 sc.

Rnds 5 and 6: Sc in each sc around.

Slip st in next sc, finish off leaving a long end.

Sew Points to Center, stuffing with polyester fiberfill before closing.

HANDLE

Rnd 1 (Right side)**:** With Pink, ch 2, 6 sc in second ch from hook; place marker to indicate beginning of rnd.

Rnd 2: 2 Sc in each sc around: 12 sc.

Rnd 3: (Sc in next 2 sc, 2 sc in next sc) around: 16 sc.

Rnd 4: Sc in Back Loop Only of each sc around ***(Fig. 3, page 46)***.

Stuff Handle with polyester fiberfill as you crochet.

Rnds 5-23: Sc in both loops of each sc around.

Slip st in next sc, finish off leaving a long end.

Sew Handle to back of Star.

Cut ribbon in half. With Pink, sew center of both pieces to top of Handle.

Side 3

SIDE 3

TREE TRUNK (Make 2)

Row 1 (Right side)**:** With Dk Brown, make 15 fhdc ***(see Foundation Half Double Crochet, page 45)***; finish off leaving a long end.

LEAVES (Make 2)

Rnd 1 (Right side)**:** With Green, ch 3, 11 dc in third ch from hook; join with slip st to top of beginning ch: 12 sts.

Rnd 2: Ch 3, dc in same st as joining, 2 dc in each dc around; join with slip st to first dc, finish off leaving a long end: 24 dc.

With **right** side facing, sew Tree Trunks to Navy Square with ends at bottom edge of Square.

With **right** side facing, sew Back Loops Only of Leaves to Square at top of Tree Trunk at different heights, leaving top edges free.

GRASS

Row 1: With Green, work 28 fdc ***(see Foundation Double Crochet, page 45)***.

Row 2 (Right side)**:** Ch 3, turn; dc in next st and in each st across; finish off leaving a long end.

With **right** side facing, sew 3 sides of Grass to bottom edge of Square, leaving top edge free.

MOON

With Lt Yellow, ch 9.

Row 1 (Right side)**:** Slip st in second ch from hook, sc in next ch, hdc in next ch, 2 dc in each of next 2 chs, hdc in next ch, sc in next ch, slip st in last ch; finish off leaving a long end.

With Black and using straight st, add eye and mouth.

With **right** side facing, sew Moon to Square, adding a straight st nose.

With White and using straight st, add stars.

Side 4

SIDE 4

GRASS

Row 1 (Right side)**:** With Lt Green, work 12 fdc.

Row 2: Ch 2, turn; skip first st, dc in next st, dc2tog, dc in next 4 sts, dc2tog twice: 8 dc.

Row 3: Ch 2, turn; beginning in first dc, dc2tog, dc in next 4 dc, dc2tog; finish off leaving a long end.

With **right** side facing, sew Grass to bottom edge of Lt Blue Square.

MUSHROOM STEM

With Dk Brown, ch 11.

Row 1 (Right side)**:** Dc in third ch from hook and in each ch across: 10 sts.

Row 2: Ch 1, turn; hdc in each st across.

Row 3: Ch 2, turn; dc in each hdc across.

Rows 4 and 5: Repeat Rows 2 and 3; at end of Row 5, finish off leaving a long end.

With **right** side facing, sew Mushroom Stem to Square on top of Grass.

MUSHROOM CAP

Row 1 (Right side)**:** With Red, ch 3, 6 dc in third ch from hook; do **not** join.

Row 2: Ch 3, turn; dc in first dc, 2 dc in each of next 5 dc: 12 dc.

Row 3: Ch 3, turn; 2 dc in next dc, (dc in next dc, 2 dc in next dc) across: 18 dc.

Edging: Ch 3, do **not** turn; work 11 dc evenly spaced across ends of rows, ch 3; working across dc on Row 3, (dc in next 2 dc, 2 dc in next dc) 6 times, ch 3; join with slip st to first dc, finish off leaving a long end.

SPOTS

CORNER

Row 1 (Right side)**:** With White, ch 3, 2 dc in third ch from hook; finish off leaving a long end.

SMALL BOTTOM

Row 1 (Right side)**:** With White and using an adjustable loop to form a ring, work 3 sc in ring; finish off leaving a long end.

SMALL

Rnd 1 (Right side)**:** With White and using an adjustable loop to form a ring, work 6 sc in ring; join with slip st to first sc, finish off leaving a long end.

SIDE

Row 1 (Right side)**:** With White, ch 3, 6 dc in third ch from hook; finish off leaving a long end.

LARGE POCKET

Rnd 1 (Right side)**:** With White, ch 3, 11 dc in third ch from hook; join with slip st to top of beginning ch: 12 sts.

Rnd 2: Ch 1, sc in same st as joining, 2 sc in next dc, (sc in next dc, 2 sc in next dc) around; join with slip st to first sc, finish off leaving a long end.

With **right** sides facing, sew Spots to Mushroom Cap, leaving top edge of Large Pocket free.

With **right** side facing, sew Mushroom Cap to Square over top edge of Mushroom Stem.

Bottom

BOTTOM MIRROR FRAME

With Grey, ch 42; being careful **not** to twist piece, join with slip st to form a ring.

Rnd 1 (Right side)**:** Ch 3, dc in next 5 chs, 2 dc in next ch, (dc in next 6 chs, 2 dc in next ch) around; join with slip st to first dc, finish off: 48 dc.

HANDLE

With Grey, ch 8.

Row 1 (Right side)**:** Dc in third ch from hook and in next 4 chs, 6 dc in last ch; working in free loops of beginning ch, dc in next 6 chs; finish off leaving a long end.

With **right** side facing, sew end of Row 1 of Handle to edge of Frame; do **not** cut yarn.

MAGIC MIRROR

Using pattern below, cut a 3" (7.5 cm) diameter circle from reflective sheet, making sure it will fit under Frame. Punch 4 evenly spaced holes around edge.

Place Frame on Pink Square to determine mirror placement. Sew mirror to Square; then with **right** side facing, sew Frame and Handle in place.

With Navy and using straight st, add design on Frame and Handle.

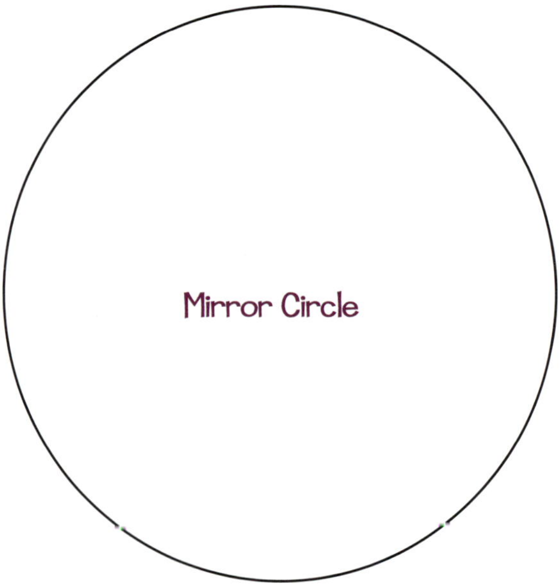

Finger Puppets

FINGER PUPPETS

OWL (Make 2)

Body (Right side)**:** With Jade, ch 3, 11 dc in third ch from hook; join with slip st to top of beginning ch: 12 sts.

Head: Skip next dc, 6 dc in next dc, skip next dc, slip st in next dc; finish off leaving remaining dc unworked.

Eyes: With White, ch 1, **tightly** ch 5, slip st in first ch, **tightly** ch 6, slip st in same ch; finish off leaving a long end.

Sew Eyes to Head.

With Black floss and using straight st, add pupils. With Lt Purple yarn and using satin st, add beak.

With **wrong** sides together and matching sts, sew pieces together leaving bottom 4 dc of Body free.

Tuft: With Jade, ch 2, slip st in st at top of Head, finish off.

Repeat for second Tuft.

WINGS & TAIL (Make 3)

With Lt Jade, ch 1, **tightly** ch 5, slip st in first ch, (**tightly** ch 6, slip st in same ch) twice; finish off leaving a long end.

Sew a Wing to each side of Body and Tail to bottom of Body.

FAIRY PRINCESS

FRONT

Head (Right side)**:** With Lt Pink, ch 3, 11 dc in third ch from hook; join with slip st to top of beginning ch, finish off: 12 sts.

Skirt: With **right** side facing, join Lt Purple with slip st in same st as joining; skip next dc, 6 dc in next dc, skip next dc, slip st in next dc, leave remaining dc unworked; finish off.

BACK

Working Head with Pink, work same as Front.

HAIR

Rnd 1 (Right side)**:** With Pink, ch 2, 6 sc in second ch from hook; join with slip st to first sc.

Row 1: (Ch 14, slip st in next sc) 3 times, leaving remaining sc unworked.

Row 2: Ch 8, turn; sc in first loop, (ch 9, sc in next loop) twice, ch 8, slip st in st at base of same loop; finish off leaving a long end.

With Black floss and using straight st, add eyes, nose, and mouth.

With **wrong** sides together and matching sts, sew pieces together leaving bottom 4 dc of Skirt free.

Arm: With Lt Pink, ch 2, 4 sc in second ch from hook; finish off leaving a long end.

Repeat for second Arm.

Crown: With Lt Yellow, ch 2, sc in second ch from hook, ch 3, sc in second ch from hook and in next ch, ch 2, sc in second ch from hook; finish off leaving a long end.

Wings

With White, ch 1, **tightly** ch 5, slip st in first ch, **tightly** ch 6, slip st in same ch: 2 loops.

Rnd 1 (Right side)**:** Work 5 sc in first loop, work 6 sc in last loop; finish off leaving a long end.

With **right** side facing, sew Arms to Skirt. Sew Wings to back of Skirt. With **right** side facing, sew Hair to Head. Sew Crown to Hair.

NATURE FAIRY

Work same as Fairy Princess, working Front Head with Lt Green and Skirt with Lt Jade.
Work Back Head with Green.

HAIR

Rnd 1 (Right side)**:** With Green, ch 2, 6 sc in second ch from hook; join with slip st to first sc.

Rnd 2: Ch 13, slip st in same st as joining, (slip st, ch 13) twice in next sc, sc in same st, 2 sc in each of last 4 sc; join with slip st to st at base of beginning ch, finish off leaving a long end.

With Black floss and using straight st, add eyes, nose, and mouth.

With **wrong** sides together and matching sts, sew pieces together leaving bottom 4 dc of Skirt free.

Arms: With Lt Green, work same as Fairy Princess.

Wings: Work same as Fairy Princess.

With **right** side facing, sew Arms to Skirt. Sew Wings to back of Skirt. With **right** side facing, sew Hair to Head.

SLEEPY FAIRY

Work same as Fairy Princess, working Front Head with Lt Jade and Skirt with Jade.
Work Back Head with Lt Purple.

HAIR

Rnd 1: With Lt Purple, ch 2, 6 sc in second ch from hook, (ch 10, slip st in same ch) 5 times; do **not** join, place marker to indicate beginning of rnd.

Rnd 2: (Sc in next sc, 2 sc in next sc) 3 times; finish off leaving a long end.

With Black floss and using straight st, add eyes, nose, and mouth.

With **wrong** sides together and matching sts, sew pieces together leaving bottom 4 dc of Skirt free.

Arms: With Lt Jade, work same as Fairy Princess.

Wings: Work same as Fairy Princess.

With **right** side facing, sew Arms to Skirt.

Sew Wings to back of Skirt.
With **right** side facing, sew Hair to Head.

GENERAL INSTRUCTIONS

ABBREVIATIONS

ch(s)	chain(s)
cm	centimeters
dc	double crochet(s)
dc2tog	double crochet 2 together
fdc	foundation double crochet(s)
fhdc	foundation half double crochet(s)
fsc	foundation single crochet(s)
hdc	half double crochet(s)
mm	millimeters
Rnd(s)	Round(s)
sc	single crochet(s)
sc2tog	single crochet 2 together
sp(s)	space(s)
st(s)	stitch(es)
tr	treble crochet(s)
YO	yarn over

SYMBOLS & TERMS

★ — work instructions following ★ as many **more** times as indicated in addition to the first time.

( ) or [ ] — work enclosed instructions **as many** times as specified by the number immediately following **or** work all enclosed instructions in the stitch or space indicated **or** contains explanatory remarks.

colon (:) — the number(s) given after a colon at the end of a row or round denote(s) the number of stitches and spaces you should have on that row or round.

Yarn Weight Symbol & Names	LACE 0	SUPER FINE 1	FINE 2	LIGHT 3	MEDIUM 4	BULKY 5	SUPER BULKY 6	JUMBO 7
Type of Yarns in Category	Fingering, size 10 crochet thread	Sock, Fingering, Baby	Sport, Baby	DK, Light Worsted	Worsted, Afghan, Aran	Chunky, Craft, Rug	Super Bulky, Roving	Jumbo, Roving
Crochet Gauge* Ranges in Single Crochet to 4" (10 cm)	32-42 sts**	21-32 sts	16-20 sts	12-17 sts	11-14 sts	8-11 sts	6-9 sts	5 sts and fewer
Advised Hook Size Range	Steel*** 6 to 8, Regular hook B-1	B-1 to E-4	E-4 to 7	7 to I-9	I-9 to K-10½	K-10½ to M/N-13	M/N-13 to Q	Q and larger

*GUIDELINES ONLY: The chart above reflects the most commonly used gauges and hook sizes for specific yarn categories.

** Lace weight yarns are usually crocheted with larger hooks to create lacy openwork patterns. Accordingly, a gauge range is difficult to determine. Always follow the gauge stated in your pattern.

*** Steel crochet hooks are sized differently from regular hooks–the higher the number, the smaller the hook, which is the reverse of regular hook sizing.

GAUGE

Exact gauge is **essential** for proper size. Before beginning your project, make the sample swatch given in the individual instructions in the yarn and hook specified. After completing the swatch, measure it, counting your stitches and rounds carefully. If your swatch is larger or smaller than specified, **make another, changing hook size to get the correct gauge**. Keep trying until you find the size hook that will give you the specified gauge.

MARKERS

Markers are used to help distinguish the beginning of each round being worked. Place a 2" (5 cm) scrap piece of yarn before the first stitch of each round, moving marker after each round is complete.

CROCHET TERMINOLOGY		
UNITED STATES		INTERNATIONAL
slip stitch (slip st)	=	single crochet (sc)
single crochet (sc)	=	double crochet (dc)
half double crochet (hdc)	=	half treble crochet (htr)
double crochet (dc)	=	treble crochet (tr)
treble crochet (tr)	=	double treble crochet (dtr)
double treble crochet (dtr)	=	triple treble crochet (ttr)
triple treble crochet (tr tr)	=	quadruple treble crochet (qtr)
skip	=	miss

BEGINNER	Projects for first-time crocheters using basic stitches. Minimal shaping.
EASY	Projects using yarn with basic stitches, repetitive stitch patterns, simple color changes, and simple shaping and finishing.
INTERMEDIATE	Projects using a variety of techniques, such as basic lace patterns or color patterns, mid-level shaping and finishing.
EXPERIENCED	Projects with intricate stitch patterns, techniques and dimension, such as non-repeating patterns, multi-color techniques, fine threads, small hooks, detailed shaping and refined finishing.

CROCHET HOOKS	
U.S.	Metric mm
B-1	2.25
C-2	2.75
D-3	3.25
E-4	3.5
F-5	3.75
G-6	4
7	4.5
H-8	5
I-9	5.5
J-10	6
K-10½	6.5
L-11	8
M/N-13	9
N/P-15	10
P/Q	15
Q	16
S	19

JOINING WITH SC

When instructed to join with sc, begin with a slip knot on hook. Insert hook in stitch or space indicated, YO and pull up a loop, YO and draw through both loops on hook.

FOUNDATION SINGLE CROCHET *(abbreviated fsc)*

Ch 2, insert hook in second ch from hook, YO and pull up a loop, YO and draw through one loop on hook **(ch made)**, YO and draw through both loops on hook **(first fsc made)**, ★ insert hook in ch at base of last fsc made, YO and pull up a loop, YO and draw through one loop on hook **(ch made)**, YO and draw through both loops on hook **(fsc made)**; repeat from ★ for each additional fsc.

FOUNDATION HALF DOUBLE CROCHET *(abbreviated fhdc)*

Ch 3, YO, insert hook in third ch from hook, YO and pull up a loop, YO and draw through one loop on hook **(ch made)**, YO and draw through all 3 loops on hook **(first fhdc made)**, ★ YO, insert hook in ch at base of last fhdc made, YO and pull up a loop, YO and draw through one loop on hook **(ch made)**, YO and draw through all 3 loops on hook **(fhdc made)**; repeat from ★ for each additional fhdc.

FOUNDATION DOUBLE CROCHET *(abbreviated fdc)*

Ch 3, YO, insert hook in third ch from hook, YO and pull up a loop, YO and draw through one loop on hook **(ch made)**, (YO and draw through 2 loops on hook) twice **(first fdc made)**, ★ YO, insert hook in ch at base of last fdc made, YO and pull up a loop, YO and draw through one loop on hook **(ch made)**, (YO and draw through 2 loops on hook) twice **(fdc made)**; repeat from ★ for each additional fdc.

ADJUSTABLE LOOP

Wind yarn around two fingers to form a ring ***(Fig. 1a)***. Slide yarn off fingers and grasp the strands at the top of the ring ***(Fig. 1b)***. Insert hook from **front** to **back** into the ring, pull up a loop, YO and draw through loop on hook to lock ring ***(Fig. 1c)*** (st made does **not** count as part of beginning ch of first rnd). Working around **both** strands, follow instructions to work sts in the ring, then pull yarn tail to close ***(Fig. 1d)***.

Fig. 1a

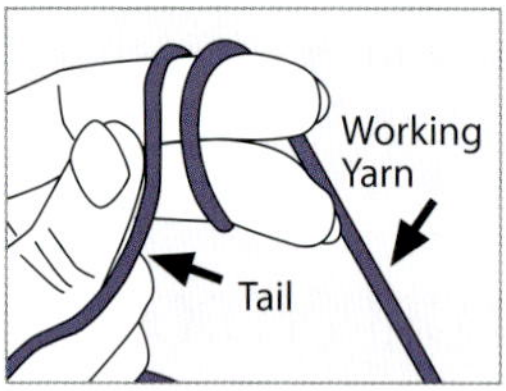

Fig. 1b

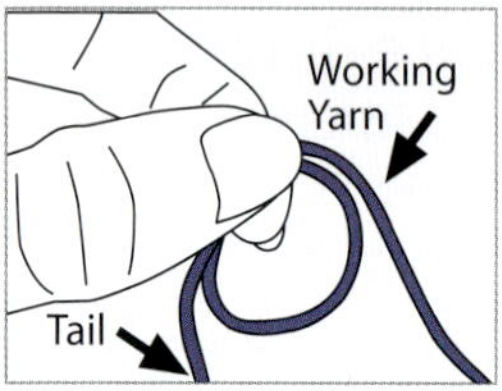

Fig. 1c

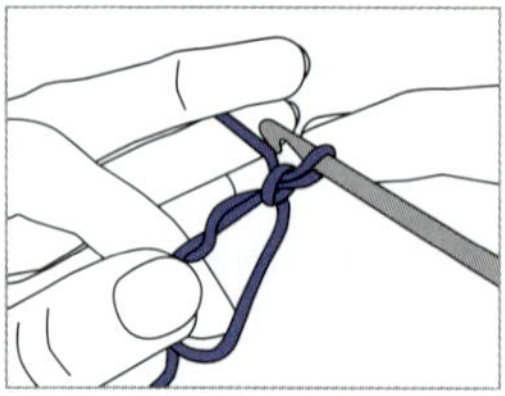

Fig. 1d

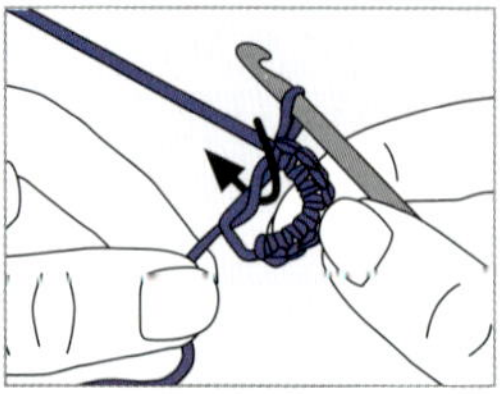

FREE LOOPS

After working in Back or Front Loops Only on a row or round, there will be a ridge of unused loops. These are called the free loops. Later, when instructed to work in the free loops of the same row or round, work in these loops ***(Fig. 2a)***.

When instructed to work in free loops of a chain, work in loop indicated by arrow ***(Fig. 2b)***.

Fig. 2a

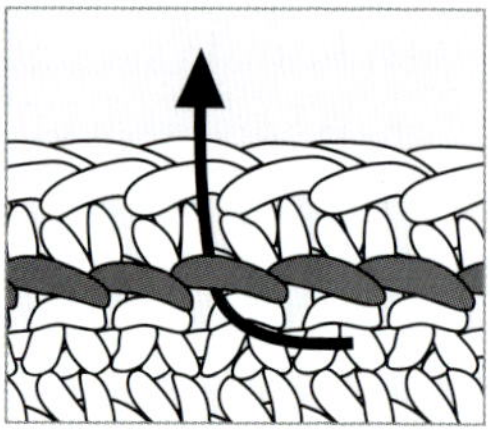

Fig. 2b

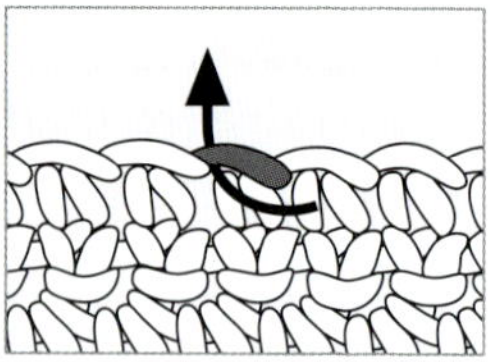

BACK OR FRONT LOOP ONLY

Work only in loop(s) indicated by arrow ***(Fig. 3)***.

Fig. 3

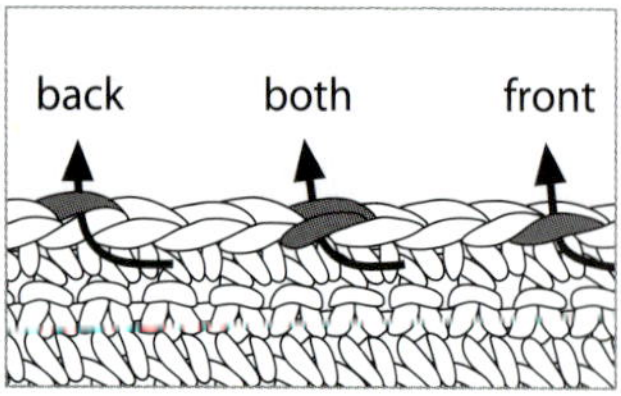

EMBROIDERY STITCHES

STRAIGHT STITCH

(abbreviated straight st)

Straight stitch is just what the name implies, a single, straight stitch. Come up at 1 and go down at 2 ***(Fig. 4)***.

Fig. 4

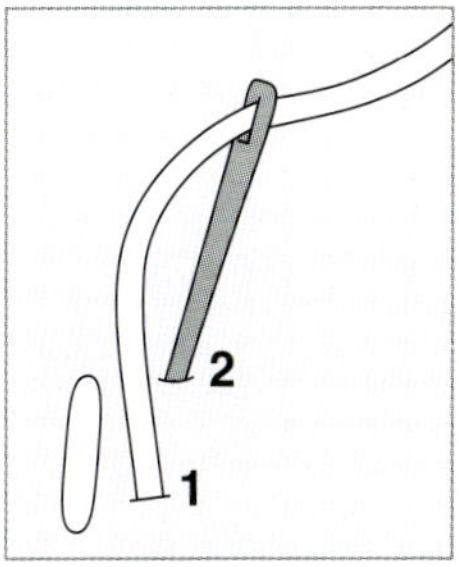

BACKSTITCH

Backstitch is worked from **right** to **left**. Come up at 1, go down at 2 and come up at 3 ***(Fig. 5)***. The second stitch is made by going down at 1 and coming up at 4.

Fig. 5

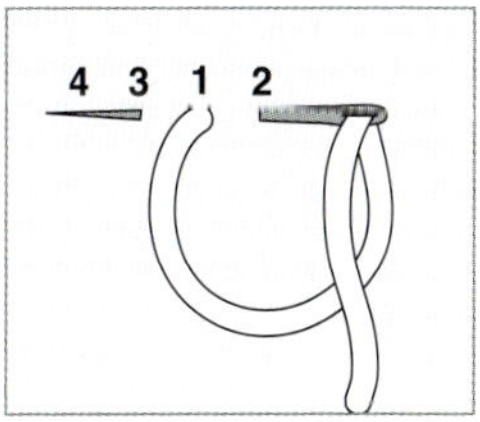

LAZY DAISY STITCH

Make all loops equal in length. Come up at 1 and make a counterclockwise loop with the yarn. Go down at 1 and come up at 2, keeping the yarn below the point of the needle ***(Fig. 6)***. Secure loop by bringing yarn over loop and down at 3. Repeat for the desired number of petals or leaves.

Fig. 6

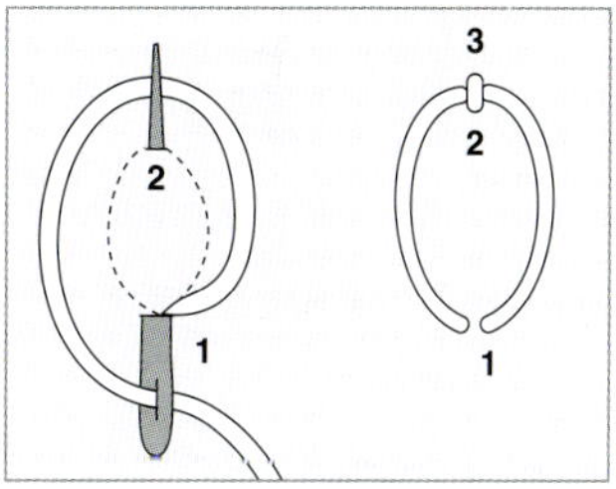

SATIN STITCH

(abbreviated satin st)

Satin stitch is a series of straight stitches that come out of and go into the same stitches. Come up at 1 and go down at 2 ***(Fig. 7)***.

Fig. 7

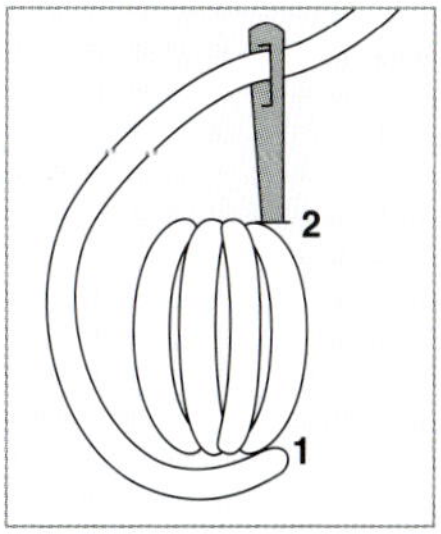

YARN INFORMATION

Each item in this book was made using Red Heart® Super Saver®, a Medium Weight Yarn. Any brand of Medium Weight Yarn may be used. It is best to refer to the yardage/meters when determining how many balls or skeins to purchase. Remember, to arrive at the finished size, it is the GAUGE/TENSION that is important, not the brand of yarn.

For your convenience, listed below are the specific colors used to create our photography models. Because yarn manufacturers make frequent changes to their product lines, you may sometimes find it necessary to use a substitute yarn or to search for the discontinued product at alternate suppliers (locally or online).

Red - #319 Cherry Red
Blue - #886 Blue
Lt Blue - #381 Lt Blue
Pink - #706 Perfect Pink
Lt Pink - #724 Baby Pink
White - #311 White
Black - #312 Black
Grey - #341 Lt Grey
Orange - #254 Pumpkin
Yellow - #324 Bright Yellow
Lt Yellow - #322 Pale Yellow
Lt Green - #625 Guava
Green - #368 Paddy Green
Purple - #776 Dk Orchid
Navy - #387 Soft Navy
Lt Purple - #579 Pale Plum
Gold - #320 Cornmeal
Dk Brown - #365 Coffee
Brown - #336 Warm Brown
Tan - #334 Buff
Lt Jade - #505 Aruba Sea
Jade - #3862 Jade
Variegated - #950 Mexicana

Production Team: Instructional/Technical Editor - Sarah J. Green; Senior Graphic Artist - Lora Puls; Photo Stylist - Lori Wenger; and Photographer - Jason Masters.